How Does a Scientist Investigate?

 HOUGHTON MIFFLIN HARCOURT

PHOTOGRAPHY CREDITS: COVER ©UpperCut Images/Alamy Images; 3 (b) ©UpperCut Images/Alamy Images; 4 (b) ©Siede Preis/Photodisc/Getty Images; 8 (inset) ©Robert Christopher/age fotostock; 8 (b) ©Corbis Flirt/Alamy Images; 9 (tr) Image Source; 10 (t) John Slater/Getty Images; 11 (b) ©Corbis Bridge/Alamy Images; 17 (t) ©JGI/Blend Images/Corbis

Printed in Mexico

ISBN: 978-0-544-07279-4

4 5 6 7 8 9 10 0908 21 20 19 18 17 16 15 14 13

4500456326   A B C D E F G

Be an Active Reader!

Look at these words.

observe	data	data table
hypothesis	microscope	bar graph
infer	graduated cylinder	
experiment	model	
variable	empirical evidence	

Look for answers to these questions.

How do scientists think about the world?

How do scientists investigate?

How do you set up an experiment?

What tools help scientists?

Why do scientists use models?

How do scientists collect data?

How do scientists display results?

Why do scientists compare results?

How do scientists think about the world?

Do you ask questions about the world around you? Scientists do! You may think like a scientist and not even know it. If you observe, or pay careful attention to, details in your world, you think like a scientist.

When scientists observe, they begin to ask questions about what they see. To find out the answer to their question, they plan an investigation. An investigation is a planned set of steps that help scientists carefully study or test something.

This student uses his senses of sight and touch to observe the rock.

How do scientists investigate?

To investigate things, all scientists follow the same general steps. Suppose you find the rock in your yard. You notice that when you scratch a rock, some parts of it crumble off. Other parts of the rock do not. You might infer that the rock is made of different materials. When you infer, you draw a conclusion.

When you think like a scientist, you ask questions about what you see. In this case, you might ask, "Do all rocks in my yard have parts that crumble when I scratch them?" Once you have a question you want to answer, you can make a plan to investigate.

What questions can you ask about the rock?

A hypothesis is a prediction about what you think will happen when you investigate.

Once you have asked a question, you can form a hypothesis. This is a suggested answer to a question that can be tested through an investigation. How can you answer a question before you investigate? You must make a good guess based on what you know. Your hypothesis might be, "Only some rocks in my yard will crumble when I scratch them."

An experiment is one type of scientific investigation. In an experiment, you test your hypothesis.

In the experiment of scratching rocks, the variable is the different types of rocks.

How do you set up an experiment?

One of the most important things about an experiment is that you must test only one variable at a time. A variable is a factor that you change in the experiment. For example, in your rock experiment, one variable might be the different types of rocks.

It's also important to test each thing in the same way. To test different kinds of rocks, you must use the same kind of tool each time and scratch each rock the same way. This will help make sure you test only one variable.

Record everything you find out by either writing it down or drawing a picture. You might even make a map of your yard to show where you found each type of rock. Everything you find out is called data.

The experiment supported your hypothesis. Only some of the rocks crumble when you scratch them.

Your hypothesis is supported! Your data show that only some of the rocks crumbled when you scratched them. Now you can draw a conclusion. That means you can use the data you collected to tell what you learned from your experiment. In this case, you draw the conclusion that different types of rocks show different results when scratched. If you wanted to, you could ask another question about why that is true, suggest a hypothesis, and run another experiment.

What if your investigation did not support your hypothesis? You can draw a conclusion that explains why. You can also plan a new investigation.

What tools help scientists?

Scientists use different tools to collect data. Some tools help you see things in greater detail. A hand lens and a microscope make things appear larger than they really are. A microscope shows details that you cannot see with your eyes alone.

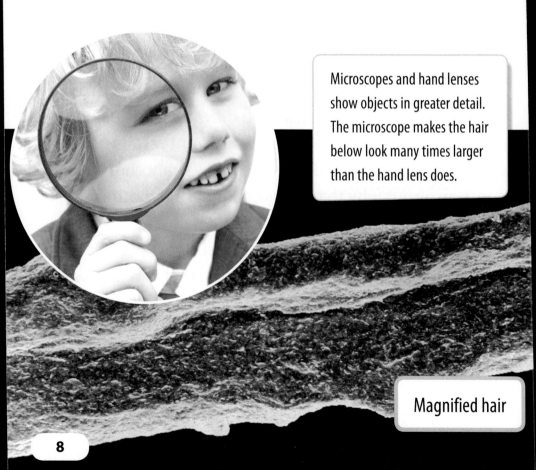

Microscopes and hand lenses show objects in greater detail. The microscope makes the hair below look many times larger than the hand lens does.

Magnified hair

The graduated cylinder has lines to mark each unit of measurement.

A thermometer is a tool for finding temperature. What things might you want to know the temperature of?

Other science tools are used for measuring. You can measure length. You can also measure volume, how much space something takes up. A ruler or meter stick measures length. A pan balance measures how much material is in an object. A graduated cylinder measures the volume of a liquid. Each tool uses different units of measurement. A thermometer measures temperature, or how hot or cold something is. There are tools to measure distance and others to measure time.

A toy car is a small model of a real car. It has the same shape and moves in a similar way.

Why do scientists use models?

There are many ways to conduct investigations. Scientists sometimes use a model to study things that are too large, too small, or have too many parts to study in nature. For example, scientists might make a model of a new bridge to study whether the design is safe. They measure the real object. Then they make a model that is much smaller. Scientists may also may look at something under a microscope and build a larger model of what they see.

No model is exactly like the real thing. For example, a model of the planets shows the order in which the planets appear in space. The model can show the size of each planet compared to the others. But a model of the planets cannot show how Earth moves around the sun. The model cannot accurately show the distances of the planets from the sun. Making models helps scientists think about questions they want to ask. Looking at a model can help a scientist form a hypothesis or make a prediction.

The model of the solar system shows which planets are larger and smaller. It cannot show exactly how far the planets are from the sun.

How do scientists collect data?

The data collected during an investigation is called empirical evidence. This is data collected based on what you observe or measure. Suppose you do an investigation and report that a plant can grow five centimeters in one week. Someone may ask, "How do you know?" You could use the empirical evidence of measurement to support your conclusion.

The number of centimeters that a plant grows in one week is part of your empirical evidence.

The lowest number on the ruler should be touching the soil. The number that is the same height as the plant is the measurement.

As a scientist, you must be careful as you collect data. When you measure a plant, do it the same way each time. Place a ruler at the top of the soil. Measure to the highest point on the plant.

It is important to record your data every time you make a measurement. You should record the data right after you have made your measurement. You can use a chart to record data. A chart puts information into rows and columns. If you measure the plant every day, you will have a lot of data to help you draw conclusions.

How do scientists display results?

One important part of doing an investigation is sharing with others what you have learned. One way you can do this is in a data table. A data table is a chart that records numbers. The left side of the table might list each week of your study. The right side of the table might show the height of your plant in centimeters. These measurements are empirical evidence that your plant is growing.

Week	Height of Plant
1	4 centimeters
2	6 centimeters
3	9 centimeters
4	12 centimeters

This data table shows the week-by-week growth of a plant.

Shade

A bar graph can make it easier to see a pattern in data. The graph can show how much the plant grew each week. The numbers on the left side of the bar graph tell you the centimeters the plant grew over time. The numbers along the bottom of the graph show the number of weeks in the experiment. Each bar tells you the height of the plant in a certain week. You can use data to help communicate your results. Data gives evidence to show whether your hypothesis is supported.

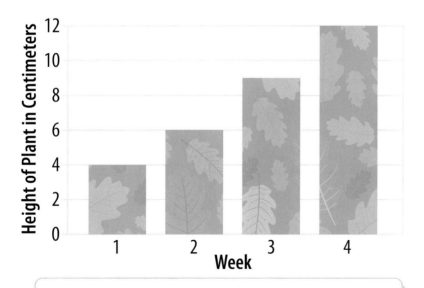

A bar graph is another way to show the number of centimeters a plant grows during the time period of the experiment.

Why do scientists compare results?

Scientists share the results of their investigations with other scientists. Another scientist may want to repeat the study. He or she may not get the exact data the first scientist did, but the results should be very similar. The conclusion of the investigation should be the same. You should also be able to repeat your own investigation and get similar results.

Sharing information about an investigation helps scientists better understand their results.

Observing nature helps scientists think of new ideas to investigate.

Sharing the results of an investigation also helps other people learn about the world. The results of one person's study can help others think of new questions. Those people can come up with new investigations. This is how real scientists work. By sharing information, one scientist may inspire the investigation of a different scientist.

Measure a Plant

Use a ruler to collect data about how a plant grows over time. Choose a plant and measure its growth after one week. Then predict how much it will grow in one month. Measure the plant once a week for four weeks. Record your data. Did your findings match your prediction?

Display Results

Use the results from the measuring investigation you did with the plant. Make a data table or bar graph to display the data. Write a short paragraph to explain whether your results matched your prediction.

Glossary

bar graph [BAHR GRAF] A graph using parallel bars of varying lengths to show comparison.

data [DAY·tuh] Individual facts, statistics, and items of information.

data table [DAY·tuh TAY·buhl] A kind of chart used for recording number data.

empirical evidence [em·PEER·i·kul EV·uh·duhns] Data collected during an investigation that can be observed.

experiment [ek·SPAIR·uh·muhnt] A test done to see whether a hypothesis is correct.

graduated cylinder [GRAJ·oo·ay·tid SIL·in·der] A container marked with a graded scale used for measuring liquids.

hypothesis [hy·POTH·eh·sis] A possible answer to a question, can be tested to see if it is correct.

infer [in·FER] To draw a conclusion about something.

microscope [MY•kroh•skohp] A tool that makes an object look several times bigger than it is.

model [MAH•dul] A representation of something real that is too big or too small or that has too many parts to be studied directly.

observe [uhb•ZERV] To use your senses to gather information.

variable [VAIR•ee•uh•bul] The one thing that changes in an experiment.